ANCIENT ROME

BY GEORGE COTTRELL

Published in 2017 by
KidHaven Publishing, an Imprint of Greenhaven Publishing, LLC
353 3rd Avenue
Suite 255
New York, NY 10010

© 2017 Booklife Publishing
This edition is published by arrangement with Booklife Publishing

Designer: Natalie Carr
Editor: Grace Jones

Cataloging-in-Publication Data
Names: Cottrell, George.
Title: Ancient Rome / George Cottrell.
Description: New York : KidHaven Publishing, 2017. | Series: Unlocking ancient civilizations | Includes index.
Identifiers: ISBN 9781534520332 (pbk.) | ISBN 9781534520356 (library bound) | ISBN 9781534520349 (6 pack) | ISBN 9781534520363 (ebook)
Subjects: LCSH: Rome–Civilization–Juvenile literature.Rome–Social life and customs–Juvenile literature.
Classification: LCC DG77.C68 2017 | DDC 937–dc23

Printed in the United States of America

CPSIA compliance information: Batch #CW17KL: For further information contact Greenhaven Publishing LLC, New York, New York at 1-844-317-7404.

Please visit our website, www.greenhavenpublishing.com. For a free color catalog of all our high-quality books, call toll free 1-844-317-7404 or fax 1-844-317-7405.

PHOTO CREDITS

ANCIENT ROME

CONTENTS

All words that appear like *this* are explained in the glossary on page 31.

ANCIENT ROME

MOST *historians* agree that the *civilization* of ancient Rome started with the founding of Rome in 753 BC. This was the beginning of ancient Rome, a civilization that would eventually control most of Europe, western Asia, and northern Africa. The ancient Roman civilization lasted for more than 1,000 years and became one of the most important civilizations in world history.

During the early days of ancient Rome, the city of Rome and its surrounding areas were founded by a mixture of people that included Latins, Greeks, and Etruscans. It was this mix of people that influenced the early culture of ancient Rome.

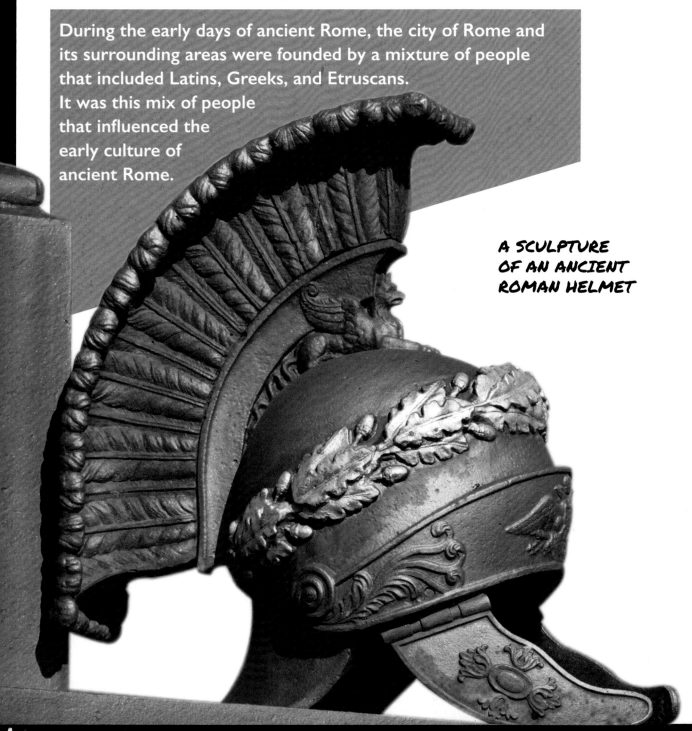

A SCULPTURE OF AN ANCIENT ROMAN HELMET

At first, ancient Rome was ruled by kings. The first, according to **legend**, was Romulus in 753 BC. Each king was **elected** by the people of Rome to rule for life and was the leader of both the Roman **government** and its religion. A group of 300 men called the Senate helped the king rule.

Historians believe there were seven kings of ancient Rome. The seventh, and last, was called Tarquin the Proud. Tarquin was hated by many due to his cruel treatment of the Roman people.

As a result, the Roman Senate and the Roman people led a *revolt* that drove Tarquin from power. This led to the formation of the Roman Republic.

THE ROMAN REPUBLIC

The Roman Republic was formed in 509 BC and lasted for almost 500 years. It brought a complicated system of government to ancient Rome that modern *democracies* still follow, and it helped ancient Rome become rich and powerful. The Roman Republic was created so no single person in Rome would ever have too much power.

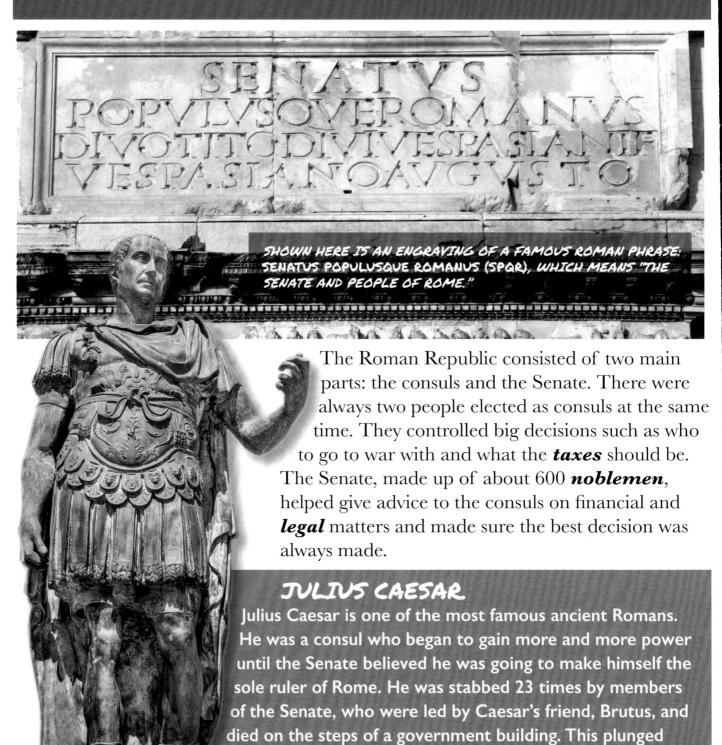

SHOWN HERE IS AN ENGRAVING OF A FAMOUS ROMAN PHRASE: SENATUS POPULUSQUE ROMANUS (SPQR), WHICH MEANS "THE SENATE AND PEOPLE OF ROME."

The Roman Republic consisted of two main parts: the consuls and the Senate. There were always two people elected as consuls at the same time. They controlled big decisions such as who to go to war with and what the **taxes** should be. The Senate, made up of about 600 **noblemen**, helped give advice to the consuls on financial and **legal** matters and made sure the best decision was always made.

JULIUS CAESAR

Julius Caesar is one of the most famous ancient Romans. He was a consul who began to gain more and more power until the Senate believed he was going to make himself the sole ruler of Rome. He was stabbed 23 times by members of the Senate, who were led by Caesar's friend, Brutus, and died on the steps of a government building. This plunged Rome into a *civil war*.

FROM REPUBLIC TO EMPIRE

In 27 BC, after many years of civil war, Octavian named himself "Augustus" and became the first emperor of Rome. This also marked the start of what we now know as the Roman Empire. It was during this first period of the Roman Empire that ancient Rome was at its most wealthy and powerful.

A STATUE OF OCTAVIAN, WHO WOULD LATER BECOME EMPEROR AUGUSTUS

The empire was able to spread thanks to the Roman army **conquering** other lands and people. However, the empire was not without its problems. There were often bad emperors, such as Nero, who almost brought disaster to ancient Rome. Nero was known for executing people who didn't agree with him and even had his own mother killed. One legend suggests that he watched as Rome burned around him. In AD 68, he killed himself when he realized that his people were about to revolt against him.

A SCULPTURE OF NERO

THE CITY OF ROME

ROME was the capital city of the ancient Roman civilization. It was the center of ancient Roman life, wealth, and power until the end of the Roman Empire. At its largest, there were more than a million people living in Rome. According to Roman legend,

Rome was founded by Romulus and Remus, the sons of the god Mars, on April 21, 753 BC. After an argument, Romulus killed Remus and named the city after himself.

The center of life in Rome was the Forum. It was a large, rectangular, public space that held great importance in Rome. It was surrounded by important buildings, such as the Senate Curia (which is where the Senate met), the Regia (the place where the original Roman kings lived), and many important temples. Important events were held at the Forum, such as trials, religious festivals, and elections.

THE RUINS OF THE TEMPLE OF ANTONINUS AND FAUSTINA NEAR THE FORUM

In major settlements, such as Rome, there would typically be a number of public buildings designed for entertainment. People would have been able to go to the theater, visit public baths, or see sporting events. The largest stadium in all of the Roman Empire was in Rome itself. Called Circus Maximus, historians believe it was built in the late 7th century BC and could hold up to 150,000 people. Romans would have watched chariot races there.

LIVING IN ROME

In Rome, as well as in other large Roman cities, people lived in one of two types of housing. Everyone other than the *upper classes* and noblemen lived in large apartment buildings called insulae. They were up to five stories high and sometimes housed up to 70 people. The upper classes lived in a kind of private home called a domus. The city of Rome was planned so that everything was built using a grid system. A grid system is where roads run at right angles to each other. This influenced other Roman cities and even modern cities such as New York.

EVERYDAY LIFE

SHOWN HERE ARE THE RESTORED RUINS OF ROMAN BATHS IN ENGLAND.

FAMILY was a very important part of everyday life in ancient Rome, even for the very rich and powerful. In early ancient Rome, the male head of the family had complete control. He could reject his children or sell them into slavery if he wanted to. Women generally had control over the family home, especially in the early years of ancient Rome, and they would look after everything that went on within it, including organizing the children's education. By the end of ancient Rome, women had even more rights, such as the ability to divorce their husbands.

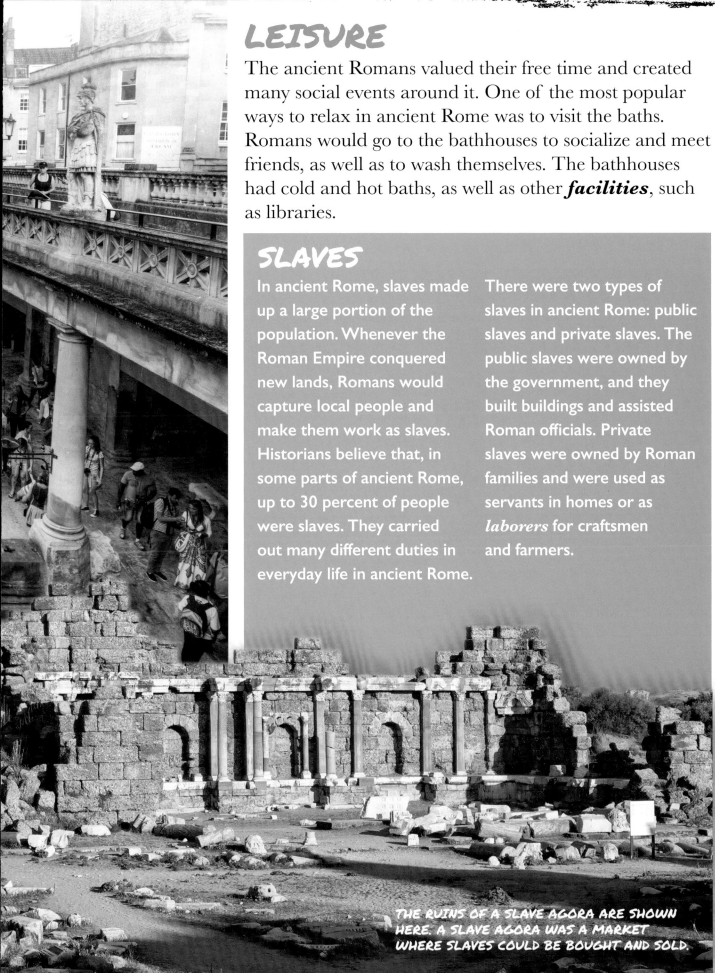

LEISURE

The ancient Romans valued their free time and created many social events around it. One of the most popular ways to relax in ancient Rome was to visit the baths. Romans would go to the bathhouses to socialize and meet friends, as well as to wash themselves. The bathhouses had cold and hot baths, as well as other *facilities*, such as libraries.

SLAVES

In ancient Rome, slaves made up a large portion of the population. Whenever the Roman Empire conquered new lands, Romans would capture local people and make them work as slaves. Historians believe that, in some parts of ancient Rome, up to 30 percent of people were slaves. They carried out many different duties in everyday life in ancient Rome.

There were two types of slaves in ancient Rome: public slaves and private slaves. The public slaves were owned by the government, and they built buildings and assisted Roman officials. Private slaves were owned by Roman families and were used as servants in homes or as *laborers* for craftsmen and farmers.

THE RUINS OF A SLAVE AGORA ARE SHOWN HERE. A SLAVE AGORA WAS A MARKET WHERE SLAVES COULD BE BOUGHT AND SOLD.

ROMAN ART AND CULTURE

ANCIENT Romans allowed art and culture to become central parts of society. This was in part because of the influence that ancient Greek art had on the Romans. They had a lot of respect for ancient Greek art and culture, especially the theater.

After they conquered Greece, they brought many Greek artists to Rome. In fact, ancient Roman art and culture were often influenced by the societies they invaded, including the Egyptians and the Celts in Britain.

THIS IS AN EXAMPLE OF AN ANCIENT ROMAN PAINTING, CALLED A FRESCO.

A BUST OF THE EMPEROR TIBERIUS

Sculptures were one of the most popular forms of art in ancient Rome. You could find them everywhere, including in businesses, parks, and people's homes. They were often busts of famous Romans. Busts are sculptures that only show the head and neck of a person. Paintings were also very popular and often painted onto the walls of homes and other buildings. Fresco painting—where the artist painted onto wet *plaster*—was the method most often used by Roman artists.

Romans liked the idea of "realism." This meant that their art tried to resemble real life as much as possible. Because of this, historians have been able to find out a lot about ancient Rome through the art of the time. It often shows scenes of normal life on pottery, mosaics, and useful everyday items. Roman art often had a practical purpose and was not only valued for the way it looked.

Culture in ancient Rome was also expressed through performances and writing. Virgil, an ancient Roman poet, wrote the *Aeneid*, which is considered to be one of the greatest epic poems ever written. In Rome, plays would be performed almost every day in public spaces such as the Forum.

A STATUE OF THE FAMOUS POET VIRGIL

GODS, GODDESSES, AND RELIGION

A S with many ancient civilizations, religion played an important role in Roman life. The Romans believed in a number of different gods and goddesses. They **worshipped** them because they believed that the gods watched over them and controlled different aspects of their lives. For instance, Neptune was the god of the seas, while Minerva was the goddess of wisdom and women's work.

A STATUE OF NEPTUNE, THE GOD OF THE SEA, WITH HIS FAMOUS TRIDENT

A MODERN PAINTING OF THE GODDESS MINERVA

The Romans were often willing to worship new gods and goddesses. This is because they thought that the new gods and goddesses would make them stronger. Because the Romans often conquered new places, they often came across new religions. For example, when the Romans invaded Egypt, they started to worship the Egyptian god Isis.

To worship the gods and goddesses, the Romans would often construct temples that were dedicated to a single god or goddess. These were large, impressive buildings. However, Romans would also have small **shrines** in their homes where they could worship the gods. The most impressive temple of all was the Pantheon in Rome. It was of such importance because it was a temple that was dedicated to all the Roman gods and goddesses.

THE CAREFULLY CONSTRUCTED CEILING OF THE PANTHEON IS SHOWN HERE.

THE PANTHEON IN ROME

CHRISTIANITY

Christianity is based around the idea that there is just one, all-powerful God. However, the Romans believed in many powerful gods. Because of this, Christians were punished and often killed by the Romans. However, as the Roman Empire spread, the amount of Christians in it grew. Eventually, in AD 313, Emperor Constantine allowed Christianity to be practiced in the Roman Empire. Ten years later, it became the official religion of the Roman Empire.

GLADIATORS

THE COLOSSEUM IN ROME

OF all the entertainment in ancient Rome, gladiator fights were the most popular. Gladiators were men who would fight each other to entertain the Roman people. They were normally slaves or prisoners, but occasionally normal Romans would volunteer as well.

Gladiators would fight in arenas called amphitheaters. Amphitheaters were the center of entertainment in Roman times. The largest amphitheater was in Rome and was called the Colosseum. It could seat 50,000 people!

THIS IS HOW THE INSIDE OF THE COLOSSEUM LOOKS TODAY. DURING ANCIENT ROMAN TIMES, IT WOULD HAVE BEEN FILLED WITH EXCITED CROWDS.

The gladiators were trained at a gladiator school to make sure that they were as entertaining as possible. They used a variety of weapons to fight, such as swords, tridents, nets, and bows. To add to the excitement, the amphitheater often contained dangerous animals from the Roman Empire, such as lions, which the gladiators had to kill.

THIS IS AN EXAMPLE OF WHAT A GLADIATOR MIGHT HAVE WORN IN THE AMPHITHEATER.

Battles between gladiators were often fought to the death. However, gladiators were allowed to beg for their life if they were about to lose. The crowd, or the emperor if he was there, would then decide if the gladiator should live or die. The few gladiators who managed to survive for a long time became very rich and famous and were often allowed to *retire*.

SPARTACUS

Spartacus is perhaps the most famous gladiator of all. He escaped from gladiator school and led an army of gladiators and slaves in a revolt against the Roman army in 73 BC. He defeated the Roman army several times before he was eventually defeated and killed in 71 BC.

THE ROMAN ARMY

THE Roman army was one of the most successful and well organized armies in all of history. It was one of the main reasons that the Roman Empire was able to rule so much of the world. The army was split into two types of soldiers—legionaries and auxiliaries.

Legionaries were Roman citizens under the age of 45 who had to fight for 25 years. They were highly trained and were paid the most money. They were taken from *tribes* that the Romans had conquered. Auxiliaries were allowed to become Roman citizens once they had fought in the Roman army for 25 years.

THIS IS HOW A LEGIONARY WOULD HAVE LOOKED.

THIS IS WHAT A TESTUDO LOOKS LIKE.
TESTUDO IS LATIN FOR "TORTOISE."

A LEGIONARY'S HELMET

Legionaries were divided into groups of 5,000 called legions. At its largest, the Roman army had 30 legions that fought all around the Roman Empire to make sure order was maintained. Including the auxiliaries, some historians believe the Roman Army had more than 1 million soldiers!

THE TESTUDO

The Roman army was very well trained. They had to practice fighting every day and be able to march 20 miles (32.2 km) in their armor. They always obeyed orders and fought in tight formations. They were famous for the testudo. This was when the Roman soldiers would lift their shields over their heads to give them protection from arrows and rocks.

ROMAN BRITAIN

BEFORE the Romans invaded, the Celts lived in Britain. The Celts were made up of several different tribes, each of which had their own leader. In Celtic Britain, there were no major towns or roads, and most people were farmers who lived in small villages and simple homes.

The Romans, led by the general Julius Caesar, first invaded Britain in 55 BC. They wanted to make Britain part of the Roman Empire. However, the Celts managed to resist, and the Romans left Britain. It was almost 100 years later, in AD 43, that the Romans, led by Emperor Claudius, invaded again and finally took control of the country.

THE RUINS OF HADRIAN'S WALL CAN BE SEEN TODAY.

The Romans called their newly conquered land Britannia. For nearly 400 years, they ruled over it. However, during the first few years of their rule, the Romans had to battle to keep control. It took them almost 30 years to gain total control over southern England.

HADRIAN'S WALL

Despite conquering southern England, northern England, and what is now Scotland, Britain was still full of *barbarians* who would *raid* the south and try to stop the Romans' plans. In AD 122, the Roman Emperor Hadrian built a wall that stretched across the middle of England. It was 73 miles (117.5 km) long and up to 20 feet (6 m) high. The wall was guarded by roughly 10,000 soldiers, and it helped stop the barbarian raids.

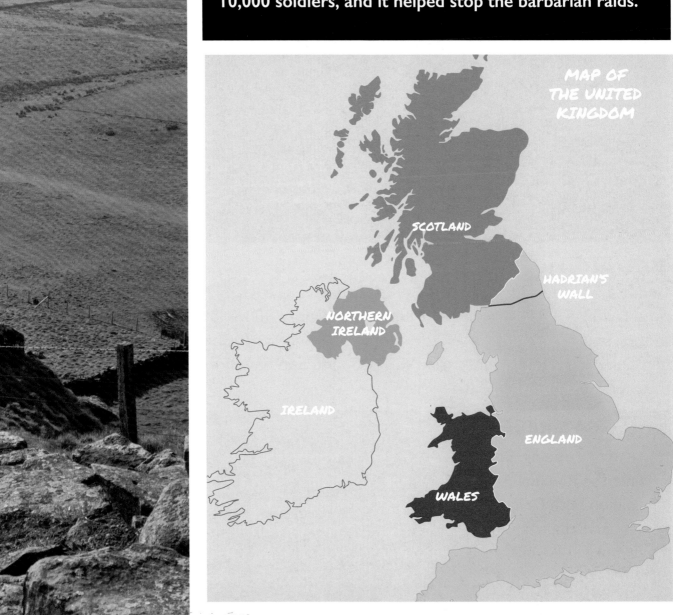

MAP OF THE UNITED KINGDOM

SCOTLAND

HADRIAN'S WALL

NORTHERN IRELAND

IRELAND

ENGLAND

WALES

LONDINIUM

In AD 50, the Romans established the city of Londinium. This later became London, England's capital city. Many of the roads that the Romans built travelled through Londinium, and it became an important center for trade. The Romans also knew that its position on the River Thames made it ideal for transporting goods between Britain and the rest of the Roman Empire.

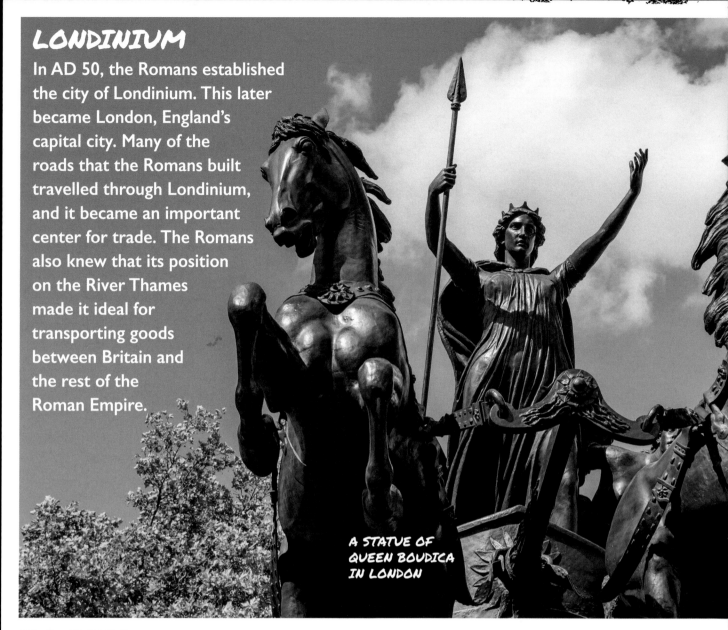

A STATUE OF QUEEN BOUDICA IN LONDON

BOUDICA

Boudica was the queen of the Iceni tribe, one of the many Celtic tribes that ruled over various parts of Roman Britain. The Romans allowed the tribes to exist as long as they paid taxes and obeyed the Romans. When her husband, King Prasutagus, died in AD 61, the Romans tried to get Boudica to pay more money to them and threatened to punish her if she didn't.

BOUDICA'S REBELLION

Instead of agreeing, Boudica led a revolt against the Romans. She marched her people on both Colchester, the capital of Roman Britain, and Londinium. Her army burned down buildings and killed hundreds of people in *protest* of the Roman rule. However, she was eventually hunted down by the well-trained Roman army. Instead of being captured, Boudica chose to drink poison and died. Boudica's rebellion was the last true resistance to Roman rule in Britain.

The Romans ended their rule of Britain in AD 410. They left because Rome and its surrounding areas were under threat from different groups of barbarians, such as the Goths and the Vandals.

YOU CAN STILL VISIT THE ROMAN BATHS IN BATH, ENGLAND, TODAY.

The legacy of the Romans in Britain can be seen even today. As well as founding London, the Romans also established many other settlements that are still important today, such as York, Bath, and Canterbury. They built hundreds of roads to connect the country and introduced the people of Britain to building with concrete. They also helped to develop many languages, the modern calendar, and the British legal system.

THE END OF ANCIENT ROME

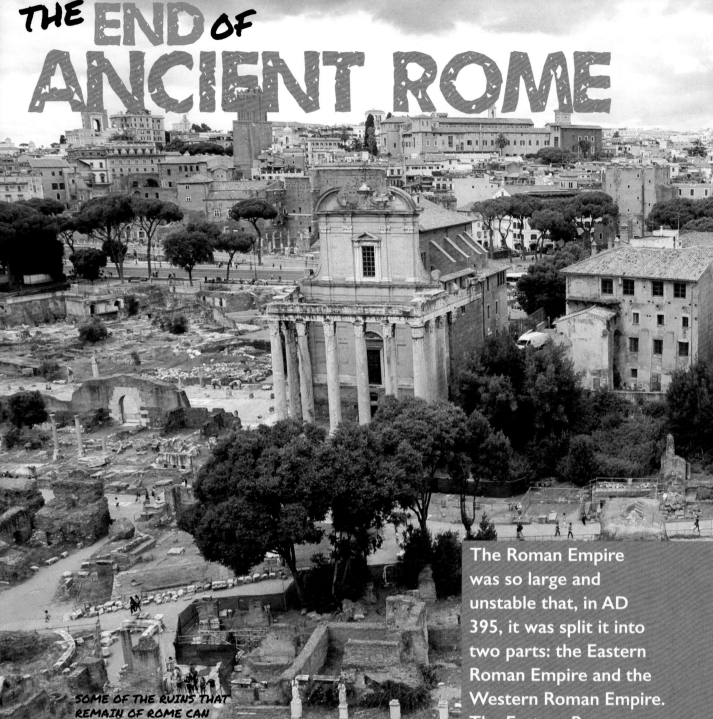

SOME OF THE RUINS THAT REMAIN OF ROME CAN STILL BE SEEN TODAY.

BY AD 200, the Roman Empire had existed for almost 1,000 years. However, by this point, its power had started to decline. This was due to the empire being too large to govern and the corruption of the politicians and leaders of Rome. Also, the Roman army was no longer as strong due to repeated attacks from tribes that surrounded the Roman Empire.

The Roman Empire was so large and unstable that, in AD 395, it was split it into two parts: the Eastern Roman Empire and the Western Roman Empire. The Eastern Roman Empire was ruled by the people in the city of Constantinople and became known as the Byzantine Empire, while the Western Empire was still ruled by emperors in Rome.

A DRAWING OF A COIN FEATURING THE FACE OF ODOACER

It was only a matter of time before the Roman Empire ended. This happened when, in AD 476, another **Germanic** barbarian tribe, led by a man named Odoacer, took control of Rome. He became King of Italy and ended the rule of the last emperor of Rome, Romulus Augustus. Most historians agree that this was the end of the Roman Empire and the ancient Romans.

THE FALL OF ROME

For hundreds of years, many people thought that the city of Rome would never be conquered. However, in AD 410, a tribe of Germanic barbarians called the Visigoths managed to finally conquer Rome. It was the first time in nearly 800 years this happened.

THE ROMAN EMPIRE

LONDON

ATLANTIC OCEAN

BLACK SEA

ROME

CONSTANTINOPLE

WESTERN EMPIRE
EASTERN EMPIRE
OTHER LAND
SEAS

THE LEGACY OF ANCIENT ROME

THE legacy of ancient Rome can still be seen today. The Romans made great progress in government, *architecture*, and the arts, and, thanks to the size of the Roman Empire, they also managed to introduce these things to millions of people around the world.

THIS ROMAN AQUEDUCT WAS USED TO TRANSPORT WATER.

Many things that we take for granted in everyday life began in ancient Rome. For instance, many legal ideas that still exist today, such as *contracts*, were used in ancient Rome.

ENGLAND'S LEGAL SYSTEM OWES A LOT TO ANCIENT ROME.

The Royal Courts of Justice

TOURISTS CAN VISIT THE COLOSSEUM IN ROME.

A ROMAN ROAD

TIMELINE OF

753 BC
◇
THE CITY OF ROME IS FOUNDED.

509 BC
◇
ROME BECOMES A REPUBLIC.

218 BC
◇
HANNIBAL INVADES ITALY.

AD 80
◇
THE COLOSSEUM OF ROME IS BUILT.

AD 122
◇
HADRIAN'S WALL IS BUILT.

AD 380
◇
CHRISTIANITY BECOMES THE RELIGION OF ANCIENT ROME.

ANCIENT ROME

73 BC

SPARTACUS LEADS A REVOLT AGAINST THE ROMAN ARMY.

55 BC

THE ROMANS INVADE BRITAIN FOR THE FIRST TIME.

44 BC

JULIUS CAESAR IS MURDERED BY A GROUP OF SENATORS.

AD 395

THE ROMAN EMPIRE IS SPLIT INTO TWO SEPARATE EMPIRES.

AD 410

THE ROMANS LEAVE BRITAIN.

AD 476

THE END OF ANCIENT ROME

MAP OF ANCIENT ROME

BRITIAIN

GAUL

IBERIAN
PENINSULAR

ITALY

ROME

MACEDONIA

GREECE

ASIA MINOR

CRETE

JUDEA

JERUSALEM

ALEXANDRIA

EGYPT

AFRICA

■ THE LANDS OF THE ROMAN EMPIRE
□ OTHER LAND
■ SEAS

GLOSSARY

architecture	the process and product of planning, designing, and constructing buildings or structures
barbarians	people who were known for being violent and not very socially or culturally advanced
civilization	a society that is very advanced
civil war	a war between people from the same country
conquering	overcoming or taking control of something by force
contracts	written or spoken legal agreements
democracies	types of government by the people
elected	chosen via a vote
facilities	places provided for particular purposes
Germanic	related to Germany or the German people
government	the group of people with the authority to run a country and decide its laws
historians	people who study history
laborers	people who do unskilled, physical work
legal	relating to law
legend	a traditional story that is typically historical, but cannot be proven to be true
noblemen	people who are part of the highest social class
plaster	a soft mixture of sand and cement, often spread on walls and ceilings
protest	an action that expresses disapproval of something, typically involving more than one person
raid	a surprise attack on an enemy
retire	to stop working for the rest of a person's life
revolt	to take violent action against a government or ruler
shrines	holy places or places of worship that are marked by buildings or other constructions
taxes	payments made to the government so it can provide services
tribes	groups of people linked by familial, social, or religious ties
upper classes	groups of people who have more money and a higher social status than most others in society
worshipped	to have expressed devotion to a god through actions or words

INDEX